Drinking Animals Coloring Book by Kitty Belle

Copyright © 2020 by Kitty Belle

All rights reserved.

No part of this book may be reproduced in any form or by any electronic or mechanical means including information storage and retrieval systems without written permission from the author, except for the use of brief quotations in a book review.

This Drinking Animals Coloring Book Belongs to

....

Table of Contents

Page 7	Irish Coffee
Page 9	Moscow Mule
Page 11	Vodka Martini
Page 13	Bees Knees
Page 15	Caipirinha
Page 17	Sidecar
Page 19	Tom Collins
Page 21	Pornstar Martini
Page 23	Piña Colada
Page 25	Gin Fizz
Page 27	Americano
Page 29	Mai Tai
Page 31	Amaretto Sour
Page 33	Dark 'n' Stormy
Page 35	French 75
Page 37	Boulevardier
Page 39	Bloody Mary
Page 41	Cosmopolitan
Page 43	Gimlet
Page 45	Espresso Martini
Page 47	Dry Martini
Page 49	Negroni
Page 51	Old Fashioned
Page 53	Margarita
Page 55	Martini
Page 57	Spirits / Liqueurs / Wines
Page 59	Spirits / Liqueurs / Wines
Page 61	Other Stuff
Page 63	Other Stuff
Page 65	Other Stuff
Page 67	Other Stuff
Page 69	Glasses
Page 71	A small favor

IRISH COFFEE

PREP TIME 10 MINS

INGREDIENTS

1 OZ DOUBLE CREAM
6 OZ FRESHLY BREWED BLACK COFFEE
2 OZ IRISH WHISKEY
1/2 - 1 TSP BROWN SUGAR AND A LITTLE PINCH OF FRESHLY GRATED NUTMEG.

PREPARATION METHOD

LIGHTLY WHIP THE CREAM. POUR THE HOT COFFEE INTO YOUR GLASS. ADD WHISKEY & SUGAR THEN STIR. GENTLY FLOAT THE CREAM ON THE TOP, SPRINKLE OVER SOME OF YOUR NUTMEG AND SERVE HOT. A NICE WARMING BOOST FOR YOUR DINNER GUESTS.

AN AFTER DINNER FAVORITE AND A SUPERBLY DECADENT FINALE TO PRETTY MUCH ANY MEAL.

MOSCOW MULE

A simple, yet classic vodka-based cocktail that was created not in Russia, but the good old U.S.A.! It was first conceived at the Cock 'n' Bull Bar in L.A. in 1941 when the bar manager supposedly had too much ginger beer in his basement and a Smirnoff salesman was trying to sell vodka to Americans. Thus, the Moscow Mule was born!

Ingredients

- 2 oz vodka
- 1/2 oz freshly squeezed lime juice
- 6 oz ginger beer.

Prep Time: 5 mins

Preparation Method

Squeeze half a lime into a Moscow Mule mug (or an old-fashioned if you don't have a copper mug) and drop in the spent shell. Add a few ice cubes, pour in the vodka, and then fill with ginger beer then serve with a stirring rod. "Заздоровье", or maybe "cheers" is a better option!

VODKA MARTINI

PREP TIME 5 MINS

INGREDIENTS

2 OZ VODKA
1/2 OZ DRY VERMOUTH
1 GREEN OLIVE OR A STRIP OF LEMON ZEST REMOVED WITH A PEELER (OR WHATEVER YOU CAN FIND LYING AROUND TO DO THE SAME JOB!).

ONE OF THE EASIEST COCKTAILS TO MAKE, EVEN IF YOU'VE HAD ONE (OR TWO) ALREADY PLUS IT'S ALSO JAMES BOND'S FAVORITE

PREPARATION METHOD

FREEZE A MARTINI GLASS FOR 15 MINUTES OR SO. FOR BOND'S FAVORITE (SHAKEN, NOT STIRRED) FILL A COCKTAIL SHAKER WITH ICE, ADD THE VODKA & VERMOUTH AND SHAKE UNTIL YOUR ARMS GIVE UP. POUR INTO A MARTINI GLASS AND GARNISH WITH AN OLIVE. OR YOU CAN HAVE IT "STIRRED" (NOT SHAKEN) - POUR THE VODKA & VERMOUTH INTO A MIXING GLASS WITH ICE. STIR VIGOROUSLY THEN POUR INTO YOUR MARTINI GLASS AND GARNISH WITH OLIVE OR LEMON PEEL. SERVE AND ENJOY AND RELEASE YOUR INNER SPY.

BEES KNEES

INGREDIENTS

2 OZ GIN
3 MAYBE 4 OZ FRESH LEMON JUICE
3 OR 4 OZ HONEY SYRUP
1/4 CUP OF (WARM) WATER

PREP TIME 5 MINS

PREPARATION METHOD

MIX WARM WATER WITH THE HONEY TO MAKE THE HONEY SYRUP. MIX UP ALL YOUR INGREDIENTS INTO A COCKTAIL SHAKER WITH A LOAD OF ICE. SHAKE UNTIL THOSE ARMS OF YOURS CAN SHAKE NO LONGER. STRAIN INTO A CHILLED COUPE GLASS AND ENJOY! THIS COCKTAIL REALLY IS THE BEES KNEES.

AN ALL-TIME CLASSIC PROHIBITION-ERA COCKTAIL.

CAIPIRINHA

INGREDIENTS

2 OZ CACHAÇA
LIME
2 TSP SUGAR

PREP TIME 5 MINS

PREPARATION METHOD

IN A DOUBLE OLD-FASHIONED GLASS MUDDLE THE SUGAR AND LIME. FILL TO THE BRIM WITH ICE, ADD THE CACHAÇA, AND STIR. GARNISH WITH YOUR LIME WHEEL. ENJOY AS MANY TIMES AS YOU LIKE TO ENHANCE THAT SAMBA VIBE!

BRAZIL'S NATIONAL DRINK AND AS CENTRAL TO BRAZILIAN CULTURE AS SOCCER, SAMBA & STREET CARNIVALS.

SIDECAR

PREP TIME 3 MINS

INGREDIENTS

1 1/2 OZ COGNAC
(GOOD COGNAC IS OBVIOUSLY BETTER!)
3/4 OZ COINTREAU
3/4 OZ OF FRESH LEMON JUICE
GARNISH WITH AN ORANGE TWIST
& SUGAR

PREPARATION METHOD

COAT THE RIM OF A COUPE GLASS WITH SUGAR.
ADD YOUR INGREDIENTS INTO YOUR SHAKER WITH SOME ICE THEN SHAKE LIKE NO ONE'S LOOKING. POUR INTO YOUR COUPE GLASS, ADD YOUR ORANGE TWIST GARNISH. GET SIPPING!.

A DIRECT DESCENDANT OF THE BRANDY CRUSTA AN OLD NEW ORLEANS BASED BEVERAGE THAT IS ENJOYING INCREASED POPULARITY IN RECENT YEARS. THE SIDECAR'S NAME REFERENCES THE MIXTURE THAT'S LEFT IN THE SHAKER AFTER STRAINING.
TO BE SERVED AS A SHOT OF COURSE.

TOM COLLINS

An all-time gin based American classic. There's still an ongoing battle for some reason as to which side of the pond it originates, but this cocktail lives up to its classic status with every single sip.

INGREDIENTS

2 oz London Dry Gin
1 oz Fresh Lemon Juice
1/2 oz Syrup
Club Soda
Lemon Wheel
Maraschino Cherry.

PREP TIME 5 MINS

PREPARATION METHOD

Add the gin, lemon juice syrup into a Collins glass. Fill to the top with ice then fill any gaps with club soda. Finish off with a lemon wheel and a maraschino cherry. Enjoy your tasty American beverage in style.

PORNSTAR MARTINI

INGREDIENTS

1 OZ VANILLA VODKA
1 PASSION FRUIT
1 OZ PASSION FRUIT LIQUEUR
(PASSOĀ IS A GOOD OPTION HERE),
1/2 TBSP LIME JUICE,
1/2 TBSP SUGAR SYRUP,
PROSECCO (OR CHAMPAGNE
IF YOU'RE SLIGHTLY MORE FLASH).

PREP TIME 8 MINS

PREPARATION METHOD

LIGHTLY WHIP THE CREAM. POUR THE HOT COFFEE INTO YOUR GLASS.
ADD WHISKEY & SUGAR THEN STIR. GENTLY FLOAT THE CREAM ON THE TOP, SPRINKLE OVER SOME OF YOUR NUTMEG AND SERVE HOT. A NICE WARMING BOOST FOR YOUR DINNER GUESTS..

ONE OF THE MOST LUSTED AFTER AND POPULAR COCKTAILS ON THE PLANET AND BEST ENJOYED WHEN THE SUN IS SHINING, AND THE SKIES ARE BLUE.

PIÑA COLADA

A 1970S ERA PUERTO RICAN SWEET SLUSHIE AND ANOTHER ALL-TIME TROPICAL CLASSIC. POSSIBLY ONE OF THE MOST WELL-KNOWN COCKTAILS ON THE PLANET.

INGREDIENTS

2 OZ LIGHT RUM
1 1/2 OZ CREAM OF COCONUT
1 1/2 OZ PINEAPPLE JUICE
1/2 OZ FRESH LIME JUICE
PINEAPPLE.

PREPARATION METHOD

STICK THE LOT INTO YOUR COCKTAIL SHAKER AND GIVE IT A GOOD OLD SHAKE. STRAIN INTO A CHILLED HURRICANE GLASS WITH CRUSHED ICE AND FINISH OFF WITH A PINEAPPLE WEDGE AND PINEAPPLE LEAF.

PREP TIME 5 MINS

GIN FIZZ

INGREDIENTS

2 OZ GIN
3/4 OZ LEMON (OR LIME) JUICE
3/4 OZ SUGAR SYRUP
2 OZ SODA WATER
(OR A LITTLE MORE IF REQUIRED).
MARASCHINO CHERRY
LEMON PEEL
OPTIONAL INGREDIENT
1 EGG WHITE.

PREP TIME 3 MINS

A OLD TIME CLASSIC WITH A LIGHT AND SOUR CITRUS FLAVOR THAT LEAVES NO HIDING OPPORTUNITIES FOR CHEAP GIN.

PREPARATION METHOD

POP YOUR INGREDIENTS INTO YOUR COCKTAIL SHAKER WITH SOME ICE AND GET SHAKING. MAKE SURE THE EGG WHITE IS MIXED IN (IF INCLUDED), STRAIN INTO A HIGHBALL GLASS STACKED WITH ICE CUBES, TOP UP WITH SODA WATER AND GARNISH WITH YOUR MARASCHINO CHERRY TO FINISH OFF IN STYLE!

AMERICANO

INGREDIENTS

1 1/2 OZ CAMPARI
1 1/2 OZ SWEET VERMOUTH
3 OZ SODA WATER (OR CLUB SODA)
LEMON TWIST (OR ORANGE TWIST FOR A CHANGE MAYBE).

PREPARATION METHOD

POUR YOUR CAMPARI AND VERMOUTH INTO AN OLD-FASHIONED GLASS FILLED WITH ICE CUBES, TOP WITH SODA AND GARNISH WITH YOUR CHOSEN CITRUS BASED FRUIT WHEEL.

WHATEVER YOU DO, DON'T CONFUSE THIS WITH AN ESPRESSO AND HOT WATER. NO WAY JOSÉ! MOSTLY SERVED BEFORE A DECENT MEAL AS AN APERITIF TO WARM UP YOUR DINNER GUESTS FOR THE CULINARY DELIGHTS THEY WILL SOON BE ENJOYING. ANOTHER JAMES BOND FAVORITE

PREP TIME 3 MINS

MAI TAI

PREP TIME 5 MINS

INGREDIENTS

1 OZ LIGHT RUM
1 OZ DARK RUM 1 OZ LIME JUICE
1/2 OZ ORANGE CURAÇAO
1/2 OZ ORGEAT SYRUP (PRONOUNCED "OR-ZAT")
1/4 OZ SIMPLE SYRUP.

GARNISH WITH LIME & MINT.

PREPARATION METHOD

CHUCK ALL OF YOUR MAIN INGREDIENTS INTO YOUR COCKTAIL SHAKER WITH SOME ICE, GET THOSE ARMS VIBRATING LIKE CRAZY, THEN POUR (NOT STRAIN) INTO AN OLD-FASHIONED GLASS. GARNISH WITH YOUR LIME UNDER MORE ICE AND THEN ADD A SPRIG OF FRESH MINT GO AND YOU'RE GOOD TO GO

NOT TO BE CONFUSED WITH THAI BOXING, ALTHOUGH THIS POPULAR AND ICONIC TIKI COCKTAIL STILL PACKS A WICKED LITTLE PUNCH. A COCKTAIL CREATED IN THE '40S IN OAKLAND, CALIFORNIA. ONE OF THE FOUNDERS OF THE TIKI COCKTAIL SCENE, VICTOR BERGERON, THREW TOGETHER SOME INGREDIENTS FOR A VISITING TAHITIAN FRIEND — UPON RECEIPT OF THE DRINK HIS FRIEND EXCLAIMED "MAI TAI - ROA AE" MEANING "OUT OF THIS WORLD — THE BEST". AND SO, THE MAI TAI NAME (ALBEIT THE SLIGHTLY SHORTER VERSION) WAS BORN!

AMARETTO SOUR

INGREDIENTS

1 1/2 OZ AMARETTO LIQUEUR
1 OZ SUGAR SYRUP
3/4 OZ LEMON JUICE
1 ORANGE SLICE
1 MARASCHINO CHERRY
ICE.

PREP TIME 5 MINS

A COMPLEX COCKTAIL THAT IS SWEET FROM THE NUTTY AMARETTO BUT ALSO VERY SOUR FROM THE LEMON JUICE. A MUST HAVE COCKTAIL OF ALL THE WORLD'S BEST BARS (AND YOUR HOUSE).

PREPARATION METHOD

POUR YOUR MAIN INGREDIENTS INTO A COCKTAIL SHAKER WITH SOME ICE AND, YES OF COURSE, GIVE IT A GOOD OLD SHAKE UNTIL EVERYTHING'S ALL MIXED UP AND NICELY CHILLED. STRAIN INTO A ROCKS GLASS OVER FRESH ICE AND GARNISH WITH A LEMON TWIST & A SKEWERED MARASCHINO CHERRY.

DARK 'N' STORMY

Sometimes simple is best and that really hits the mark with this cocktail masterpiece. Made with Gosling's (and only Gosling's) Black Seal Rum (the "dark") and ginger beer (the "stormy"). Probably the cocktail with the coolest name too. FYI, it's mostly frowned upon to liven up a D 'N' S with lime juice, but this can sometimes be an option.

INGREDIENTS

Gosling's Black Seal Rum
Ginger Beer
Lime Wedge.

PREP TIME 3 MINS

PREPARATION METHOD

Fill up a highball glass with ice cubes and add the rum. Mix in your ginger beer and stir. Garnish with a lime wedge for a classy finishing touch. Release your inner pirate!

FRENCH 75

INGREDIENTS

2 OZ CHAMPAGNE
1/2 OZ LEMON JUICE
1 OZ LONDON DRY GIN
(IF YOU HAVE IT)
SUGAR.

PREPARATION METHOD

ADD YOUR GIN, A PINCH OF SUGAR AND CRACKED ICE INTO YOUR COCKTAIL SHAKER AND SHAKE HARD. STRAIN INTO A COLLINS GLASS HALF-FULL OF ICE. TOP OFF WITH YOUR CHAMPAGNE. FEEL IMMEDIATELY STYLISH AND SLIGHTLY FRENCH AT THE SAME TIME. BON APPETIT.

PREP TIME 5 MINS

A CLASSY COCKTAIL DATING BACK TO PRE-WW1 TIMES. IT ORIGINATED AT THE NEW YORK BAR IN PARIS IN 1915. IN FRANCE IT'S JUST CALLED IT A "SOIXANTEQUINZE".

BOULEVARDIER

INGREDIENTS

1 OZ BOURBON OR RYE WHISKEY
1 OZ CAMPARI
1 OZ SWEET VERMOUTH
GARNISH WITH ORANGE TWIST
OR MARASCHINO CHERRY.

THIS CLASSIC COCKTAIL LITERALLY MEANING "A MAN ABOUT TOWN" WAS CREATED BY ERSKINE GWYNNE, THE PUBLISHER OF "BOULEVARDIER" – A MAGAZINE FOR EXPATS LIVING IN PARIS IN THE 1920S. THE BOULEVARDIER IS WIDELY PRAISED FOR ITS DELICATE BALANCE OF BITTER, BOOZY AND SWEET AROMAS. BEST SERVED WITH A GOOD QUALITY SPIRIT AND VERMOUTH. A RICH AND INTRIGUING COCKTAIL AND CLEVERLY NAMED.

PREPARATION METHOD

ADD YOUR MAIN INGREDIENTS INTO A MIXING GLASS WITH ICE AND STIR WELL. STRAIN INTO AN OLD-FASHIONED GLASS OVER FRESH ICE. GARNISH WITH ORANGE PEEL OR A MARASCHINO CHERRY TO COMPLETE THIS SOPHISTICATED AND HANDSOME COCKTAIL.

PREP TIME
3 MINS

BLOODY MARY

A vodka-based hair of the dog and nutritional breakfast all in one! Perhaps one of the most versatile cocktails that can also be enjoyed with your brunch.

INGREDIENTS

2 oz vodka
4 oz tomato juice
1 lemon wedge
1 lime wedge
2 dashes of tabasco sauce
2 tsp prepared horseradish
2 dashes of worcestershire sauce
A pinch of celery salt
A pinch of ground pepper
A pinch of smoked paprika
Garnish with a lime wedge
Green olive,
A sprig of parsley and an optional celery stalk

PREPARATION METHOD

Pour a pinch of celery salt onto a small plate. Kiss (rub around the rim) a pint glass with a lemon or lime wedge then roll the outer edge of the pint glass with the celery salt until fully covered then fill with ice and set aside for now. Squeeze your lemon & lime wedges into a cocktail shaker then drop them in too. Add the rest of your ingredients and some ice and shake gently (for a change). Strain into your glass and finish with your parsley sprig, a couple of speared green olives, lime wedge and your (optional) celery stalk. Sounds complicated, but it's actually reasonably easy and you'll be rewarded handsomely for your troubles.

PREP TIME 5 MINS

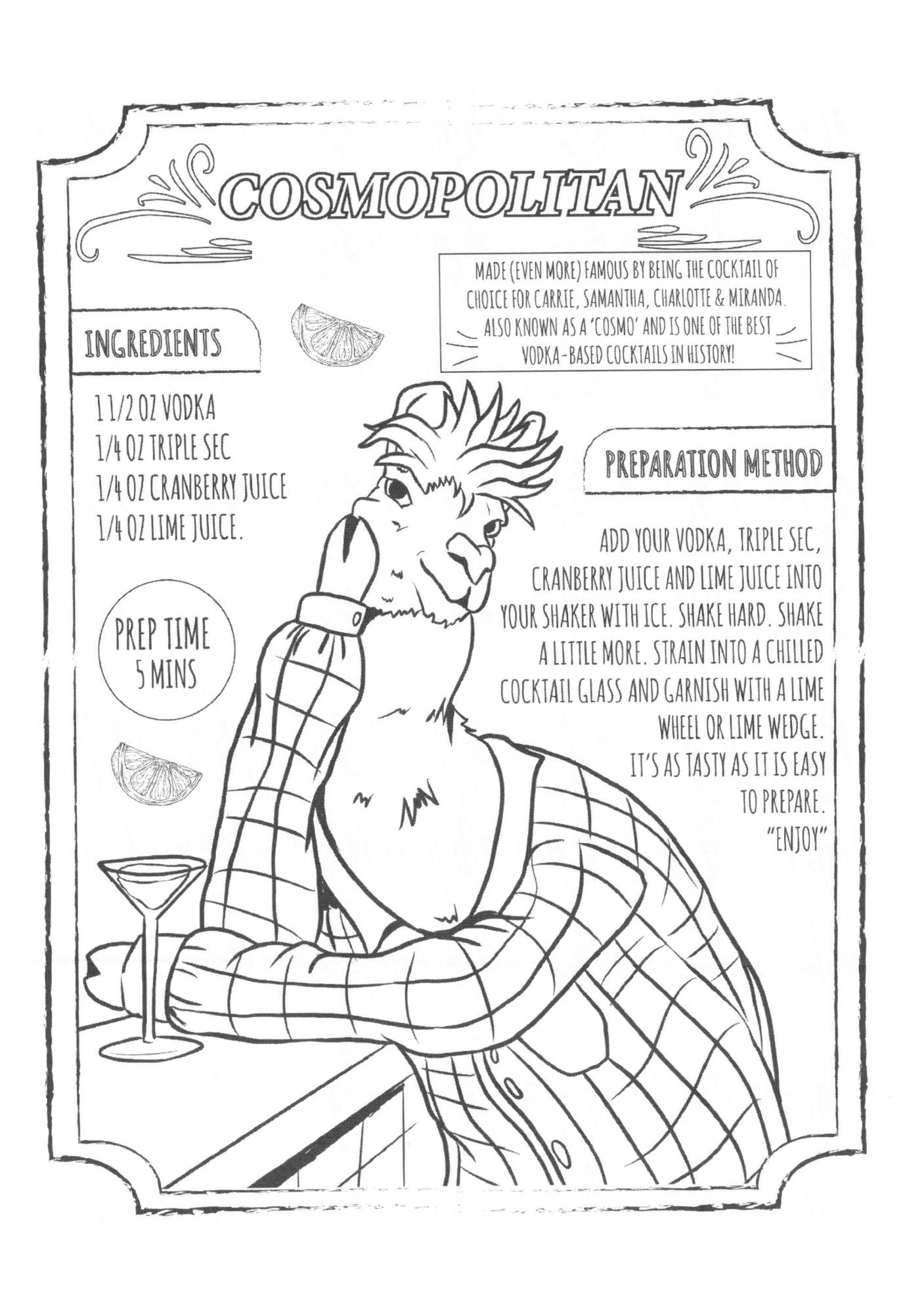

COSMOPOLITAN

Made (even more) famous by being the cocktail of choice for Carrie, Samantha, Charlotte & Miranda. Also known as a 'Cosmo' and is one of the best vodka-based cocktails in history!

INGREDIENTS

1 1/2 oz Vodka
1/4 oz Triple Sec
1/4 oz Cranberry Juice
1/4 oz Lime Juice.

PREP TIME 5 MINS

PREPARATION METHOD

Add your vodka, triple sec, cranberry juice and lime juice into your shaker with ice. Shake hard. Shake a little more. Strain into a chilled cocktail glass and garnish with a lime wheel or lime wedge. It's as tasty as it is easy to prepare.
"Enjoy"

GIMLET
(PRONOUNCED WITH A HARD "G")

THE GIMLET IS NAMED AFTER THE SMALL, SHARP TOOL USED TO PIERCE AND TAP BARRELS OF BOOZE ON BOARD A SHIP – WITH THE DRINK HAVING A SIMILAR SHARP, PIERCING EFFECT. THE OTHER SUGGESTION IS THAT IT IS NAMED IN HONOR OF THE BRITISH ROYAL NAVAL SURGEON REAR-ADMIRAL SIR THOMAS GIMLETTE KCB WHO ADDED LIME TO GIN RATIONS AS A PREVENTATIVE MEASURE TO WARD OFF SCURVY. EITHER WAY, THE BACK STORY IS AS GOOD AS THIS PIERCING MEDICINAL COCKTAIL.

INGREDIENTS

2 1/2 OZ GIN
1/2 OZ FRESH LIME JUICE
1/2 OZ SUGAR SYRUP
LIME WHEEL.

PREP TIME 5 MINS

PREPARATION METHOD

ADD YOUR INGREDIENTS INTO YOUR SHAKER WITH PLENTY OF ICE. GET SHAKING, THEN STRAIN INTO AN OLD-FASHIONED GLASS FILLED WITH ICE. GARNISH WITH YOUR LIME WHEEL. AHOY, ME HEARTIES!

ESPRESSO MARTINI

Like a refined vodka and Red Bull, but for coffee aficionados. A cocktail that promises a delicious lift, while also offering a calming effect to continue your buzz. Sometimes also referred to as a vodka espresso.

INGREDIENTS

2 oz vodka
1/2 sugar syrup
1/2 coffee liqueur
1 oz freshly brewed espresso
Coffee beans.

PREPARATION METHOD

Add your main ingredients into your shaker along with some ice and give it a good old shake. Strain into a chilled cocktail glass then garnish with 3 coffee beans. Enjoy the ride(s).

PREP TIME
3 MINS

DRY MARTINI

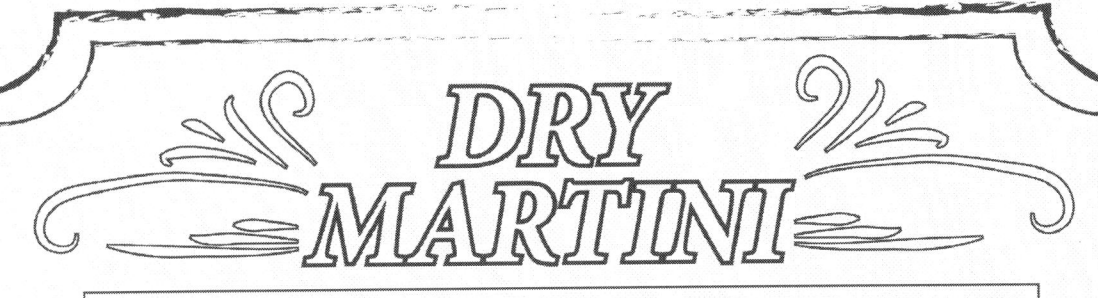

Another all-time classic cocktail that hails back to the mid 19th century. It is commonly suggested that the martini was created for a miner who struck gold. The miner wanted to celebrate with champagne, but there was none. The bar tender then put together some ingredients he had from behind the bar and the martini was born!

INGREDIENTS

2 1/2 oz gin
1/2 oz dry vermouth
1 dash of orange bitters
Lemon twist.

PREPARATION METHOD

Add your ingredients into a mixing glass with ice and get stirring. Strain into a chilled cocktail glass, then finish with a lemon twist garnish.

PREP TIME
3 MINS

NEGRONI

INGREDIENTS

1 OZ GIN
1 OZ CAMPARI
1 OZ SWEET VERMOUTH
AN ORANGE.

PREP TIME 3 MINS

PREPARATION METHOD

ADD YOUR INGREDIENTS INTO A MIXING GLASS WITH ICE AND STIR UNTIL FULLY MIXED. STRAIN INTO A ROCKS GLASS FILLED WITH ICE AND GARNISH WITH AN ORANGE TWIST. SALUTI!

ONE OF THE WORLD'S MOST REGULARLY ORDERED COCKTAILS. A TRIPLE INGREDIENT ITALIAN COCKTAIL THAT OFFERS A HUGE VARIETY OF DIFFERENT OPTIONS THROUGHOUT THE NEGRONI FAMILY TREE THAT ARE ALWAYS OPEN TO INNOVATION. SHOULD ALWAYS BE SERVED 1/3, 1/3 AND 1/3 EQUAL MEASURES.

OLD FASHIONED

PREP TIME 3 MINS

As the name suggests, this one is a bonafide classic that never stops oozing coolness. It's the cocktail that started it all with its four humble ingredients being put together alongside the first printed use of the word "cocktail". The world's oldest and most popular cocktail – fact!

INGREDIENTS

2 OZ RYE OR BOURBON,
2 DASHES OF ANGOSTURA BITTERS
CLUB SODA
1 SUGAR CUBE.

PREPARATION METHOD

Put your sugar cube into an old-fashioned glass then wet it down with angostura bitters and a little dash of club soda. Crush the sugar cube with a wooden muddler then rotate the glass to equally line the base of the glass. Add your ice and chosen whiskey then finish off with an orange twist. Add a stirring rod too if you're going for additional style points.

MARGARITA

INGREDIENTS

2 OZ TEQUILA
1 OZ COINTREAU
1 OZ LIME JUICE
SALT.

Probably the most well-known cocktail in the world. Margarita, meaning "daisy" in Spanish hails from Mexico and grew in popularity when the U.S. made it illegal to drink alcohol within its borders. So, crafty and thirsty Americans immediately went south of the border to Mexico to get their alcohol fix.

PREPARATION METHOD

Chill a lowball glass then rub (kiss) its rim with a lime, then dip into some coarse salt. Add your ingredients into your cocktail shaker with some ice and give it a good old shake. Strain into your lowball over ice and pop in your lime wedge. Salud!

PREP TIME
3 MINS

MARTINI

We finish with another gin-based cocktail, but one that is the most famous of all. The Martini is also the cocktail that generates most arguments as to how it should be prepared to make it the "perfect" martini and is, truly an accomplishment rare to behold if you can pull this off.

INGREDIENTS

2 oz gin
1/2 oz dry vermouth
Lemon zest.

PREPARATION METHOD

Pour your gin and vermouth into a cocktail shaker with some ice. Give it a good old shake. Strain into a chilled martini glass then garnish with lemon zest. Cocktail perfection (possibly).

PREP TIME 3 MINS

SPIRITS/LIQUEURS
WINES

AMARETTO LIQUEUR
ITALIAN FOR "LITTLE BITTER". IT'S A SWEET ITALIAN LIQUEUR MADE FROM BITTER ALMONDS THAT CAN BE CONSUMED ON ITS OWN OR CAN BE USED FOR SEVERAL CULINARY APPLICATIONS

BOURBON WHISKEY
A TYPE OF AMERICAN WHISKEY THAT IS DISTILLED FROM GRAIN MASH AND AGED FOR A MINIMUM OF 2 YEARS. HAILING FROM BOURBON, KENTUCKY.

CACHAÇA LIME
SOMETIMES ALSO KNOWN AS 'CANINHA' A BRAZILIAN RUM MADE FROM SUGAR CANE.

CAMPARI
AN ALCOHOLIC LIQUEUR, CHARACTERIZED BY ITS DARK RED COLOR DERIVED FROM INFUSING HERBS, FRUIT, ALCOHOL AND WATER WHICH ORIGINATED IN ITALY

COFFEE LIQUEUR
A DRINK MADE FROM DISTILLED SPIRITS, SUGAR AND COFFEE USED OFTEN IN COCKTAILS OR TAKEN NEAT, OVER ICE.

COGNAC
A VARIETY OF BRANDY NAMED AFTER THE COMMUNE OF COGNAC, FRANCE.

SPIRITS/LIQUEURS WINES

COINTREAU
A colorless French orange-flavored triple sec liqueur often consumed as an apéritif or as a digestif.

GOSLING'S BLACK SEAL RUM
Gosling's signature 80 proof Bermuda black rum.

IRISH WHISKEY
Whiskey from Ireland! The word 'whiskey' from Gaelic means 'water of life'.

LONDON DRY GIN
A juniper-based spirit from the capital of England!

RYE WHISKEY
See "Bourbon Whiskey". It's pretty much the same thing.

TEQUILA
A distilled beverage made from the blue agave plant that offers a pure semi-sweet taste. Often consumed neat but often taken with salt and lime.

VERMOUTH
An aromatized fortified wine flavoured with various botanicals.

VODKA
A clear distilled alcoholic beverage composed mainly of water and ethanol origination from Poland and Russia.

OTHER STUFF

ANGOSTURA BITTERS
CONCENTRATED BITTERS BASED ON GENTIAN, HERBS AND VARIOUS SPICES USED OFTEN FOR FLAVORING FOOD AND BEVERAGES.

CELERY SALT
A SEASONED SALT MADE FROM GROUND CELERY SEEDS.

COFFEE
A BREWED DRINK PREPARED FROM ROASTED COFFEE BEANS

CREAM
A DAIRY PRODUCT SKIMMED FROM THE TOP OF MILK BEFORE HOMOGENIZATION.

CREAM OF COCONUT
AN OPAQUE MILKY-WHITE LIQUID TAKEN FROM THE GRATED PULP OF MATURE COCONUTS.

ESPRESSO
AN ITALIAN COFFEE MAKING TECHNIQUE WHERE A SMALL AMOUNT OF NEARLY BOILING WATER IS FORCED UNDER PRESSURE (EXPRESSED) THROUGH FINELY GROUND COFFEE BEANS.

GINGER BEER
A SWEETENED AND CARBONATED USUALLY NON-ALCOHOLIC BEVERAGE MADE WITH GINGER SPICE, YEAST AND SUGAR.

GROUND PEPPER
THE FLOWERING VINE OF THE PIPERACEAE, KNOWN AS A PEPPERCORN, THAT HAS BEEN GROUND.

OTHER STUFF

HORSERADISH
A root vegetable that's related to mustard, wasabi, broccoli and cabbage that is often used as a spice or condiment.

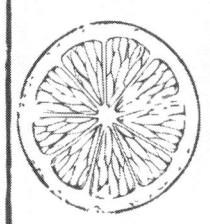

ICE CUBE
Water than has been put in the freezer until it changes from a liquid to a solid form. Can be in a cube or crushed or cracked depending on preference. Used pretty much in the preparation of every chilled cocktail.

LIME WHEEL
Garnish made by cutting a cross section of fresh lime about 1/4 inch thick.

LIME WEDGE
Slice about a 1/4 inch off each end of your lime, then cut in half lengthwise. Place your lime face down on your chopping board then slice at an angle lengthwise again to create the perfect wedge.

LEMON ZEST
The outer skin of a lemon that you can extract using a vegetable peeler, paring knife or maybe even an old-fashioned box grater.

LIME SHELL
Half a lime that has been hollowed out with a reamer to create a bowl that floats in your drink.

MARASCHINO CHERRY
A preserved sweetened cherry usually made from light-colored sweet cherries.

MINT
An aromatic plant used to create a lingering cooling effect on the tongue.

OTHER STUFF

NUTMEG
THE SEED OR GROUND SPICE FROM THE MYRISTICA GENUS OF TREES THAT GIVES A SWEET AND DELICATE FLAVOR.

OLIVE
THE FRUIT OF THE 'OLEA EUROPAEA' MEANING EUROPEAN OLIVE. A SMALL, USUALLY GREEN FRUIT WITH A SALTY AND SAVORY TASTE AND A SLIGHTLY OILY TEXTURE.

ORANGE BITTERS
A COCKTAIL FLAVORING MADE FROM THE PEELS OF SEVILLE ORANGES, CARDAMOM, CARAWAY SEED CORIANDER, ANISE AND BURNT SUGAR.

ORANGE TWIST
A THIN PIECE OF ORANGE PEEL USED TO ENHANCE THE FLAVOR WITH THE ADDITION OF CITRUS OILS.

SALT
A MINERAL COMPOSED MAINLY OF SODIUM CHLORIDE USED FOR VARIOUS CULINARY USES.

SIMPLE SYRUP OR SUGAR SYRUP
IT'S BASICALLY SUGAR AND WATER, THAT'S IT. HEAT UP 1 CUP OF WATER AND 1 CUP OF SUGAR AND ALLOW TO SIMMER UNTIL DISSOLVED. ALLOW TO COOL AND YOU'RE ALL DONE. YOU CAN THEN SYPHON INTO A WELL-SEALED BOTTLE, PLACE IN YOUR REFRIGERATOR AND IT WILL KEEP UNTIL YOUR NEXT COCKTAIL PARTY! ADD EXTRA SUGAR FOR ADDITIONAL THICKNESS OR SWEETNESS IF DESIRED.

STIRRING ROD
A THIN ROD USE TO STIR COCKTAILS IN CASE THE INGREDIENTS HAVEN'T MIXED WELL ENOUGH

TOMATO JUICE
LITERALLY JUST THE JUICE FROM A TOMATO.

OTHER STUFF

TABASCO SAUCE
A BRAND OF HOT SAUCE MADE FROM TABASCO PEPPERS, VINEGAR AND SALT. A CUPBOARD ESSENTIAL.

WOODEN MUDDLER
A BARTENDER'S TOOL USED TO MUDDLE FRUITS HERBS AND SPICES IN THE BOTTOM OF A GLASS.

WORCESTERSHIRE SAUCE
A FERMENTED SAUCE MADE FROM MALT VINEGAR, MOLASSES, SUGAR, SALT, ANCHOVIES, TAMARIND, ONIONS, AND GARLIC. FROM WORCESTER, ENGLAND.

MEASUREMENTS

1 OZ = 30 ML (PRETTY MUCH)

1 TSP = 1 TEASPOON

1 TBSP = 1 TABLESPOON

GLASSES

COUPE GLASS
A stemmed glass featuring a broad shallow bowl

MARTINI GLASS
A stemmed glass with an inverted cone bowl

COCKTAIL SHAKER
A device used to mix beverages.

COLLINS GLASS
A long glass tumbler

HIGHBALL GLASS
A tall glass tumbler that typically contains 8 to 12 oz. Taller than an old-fashioned glass, but shorter and wider than a Collins glass.

HURRICANE GLASS
A taller drinking glass that typically contains around 20 oz of fluids. Usually used to serve mixed drinks.

OLD-FASHIONED GLASS
A short tumbler used for serving spirits

MOSCOW MULE COOPER MUG
Yes, it's not a glass, that's correct. It's a copper mug used to serve Moscow mules! The mug typically takes on the cold temperature of the liquid.

PINT GLASS
A large conical glass made to hold a British imperial pint which is equivalent to 20 oz in real terms.

A small favour

Hello and thank you for purchasing this Drinking Animals Coloring Book!

I really hope you had a great time coloring in the fun drinking animals and that you also enjoyed sharing a cocktail (or two) with your friends along the way!

If you enjoyed the book it would really be cool if you could give an honest review so that you can share your experience with others. I really try hard to create great books for everyone to enjoy and a great review really helps with my motivation to keep writing and creating more cool books.

And if you didn't enjoy it (boo to you) then just close off this page and keep moving...

By the way, if you are feeling stressed with life I do have two other great books that you might enjoy:

Killer Cats - A Stress Relieving & Relaxation Coloring Book For Cat Loving Adults With A Sense Of Humor.

US: www.amazon.com/dp/B087SCCYM9
UK: www.amazon.co.uk/dp/B087SCCYM9

Or there's also:

The Curious Healing Properties of Coloring - A cheeky but relaxing alternative coloring book for adults.

US: www.amazon.com/dp/B089D1G9GB
UK: www.amazon.co.uk/dp/B089D1G9GB

Thanks again and take care,

Kitty B xoxo

Made in the USA
Columbia, SC
05 November 2024